Squeeze

Poems from a Juicy Universe

by Heidi Mordhorst

Photographs by Jesse Torrey

WORDSONG

BOYDS MILLS PRESS

To my mother and father, who expected everything
and to Lucy, Erika, and Robin, who showed up
every other Wednesday expecting something
– H. M.

To Dan, Jack, and Anna
– J. T.

Text copyright 2005 by Heidi Mordhorst
Photographs copyright 2005 by Jesse Torrey

Published by Wordsong
Boyds Mills Press, Inc.
A Highlights Company
815 Church Street
Honesdale, Pennsylvania 18431
Printed in China

Publisher Cataloging-in-Publication Data (U.S.)
Mordhorst, Heidi.
Squeeze : poems from a juicy universe / Heidi Mordhorst ; photographs by Jesse Torrey.
p. cm.
ISBN 1-59078-292-5 (alk. paper)
1. Children's poetry, American. I. Torrey, Jesse, 1969- II. Title.

PS3613.O717S67 2005
811'.6—dc22

2004030659

Designed by April Ward

First edition, 2005

10 9 8 7 6 5 4 3 2 1

Contents

Squeeze 5

Early Bird 6

Honeysuckle Hunting 7

Stuck in a Hug 8

A Purple Place 9

Throwing the Roads 10

Inventing the Tactoscope 11

So Delicious It Makes You Want to Dance 12–13

Birdseed 14–15

Launch 16

Singing the Swing 17

Independence Day Graffiti 18

There, Yet 19

How to Run Away 20–21

Stop for Horses on Bridge 22

What I Wanted and What I Got 23

Deep End 24

Down Under Florida 25

Backseat Breeze 26

Rooftop 27

The Moon Moves 28–29

The Skin Giver 30

Thinking Wrinkles 31

Falling 32

Squeeze

Wherever you are
is somewhere sour or sweet—
a lemon heaven
full of juice to squeeze.

Some days sting
and others pour like sugar
from your spoon.

This lemon heaven isn't high or blue
but here, and yellow,
and you,
only you,
are holding it in your hand.

Early Bird

It's the noise and quiet that wake you up,
the silent din of dawn:
birdtalk and cicadabuzz
where schoolbus grind should be.

It's the light all dim in one window,
brighter in the other:
skyshade and sunblush
reminding you which way's east.

It's the reeling feeling that you're the first
into the newborn day:
clockstop and bodyfreeze
while you choose which way to leap.

Honeysuckle Hunting

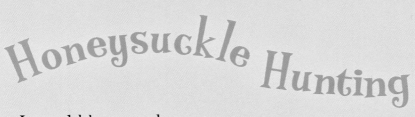

It could be anywhere.
We stand stock still and sniff
the green breathing of daisy, vine and leaf.

Ears pricked and noses high,
we listen for the drowsy hum
of yellow golden honey.

There, on the fence!
We'll steal it from the bees,
pluck a tiny trumpet blossom,

pinch the end with finger and thumb,
like biting the vanilla-dripping tip
of an ice-cream cone.

Slowly, slowly, draw it out—
pull the stamen through, tongue poised
to catch one crystal drop of sweetness.

Stuck in a Hug

"Snug as a bug in a hug,"
says Gran, like she always does,
and laughs down my neck
with her smoky-mint breath.

But I'm not just snug—
I'm squashed and I'm squeezed
and I can't quite breathe,
stuck inside this hug.

She holds me tight for half a year,
and I hang there, pinned,
and wait for War—how Gran
sticks out her chin and squints,

plays her cards like a hurricane
and never lets me win.
Her hug ends and then I'm free!
I hug back, and start the game.

A Purple Place

Purple is an inside color,
like the lining of a cape—
   like the dusky
   like the musky
inside of a hiding place.

A purple place all lined with dust
that I didn't know was here—
   a certain place
   a curtain place
behind my granddad's heavy chair.

And when I'm in this purple place
my heartbeat is the only sound—
   inside the plush
   inside the hush
what's inside me rushes out

Throwing the Roads

This is the rule for Throwing the Roads:
we gather the rug up into a knot,
toss it high and let it fall—and so it stays.
We don't nudge or yank or rearrange,
but sit and survey the lay of our land,
its cliffs and valleys, rivers and rifts.

Fix the compass on High Point Peak
to see where the eastern sun will rise;
and west, where the rug lies flat and smooth,
these are our fields and pastures.
Set the tractor out to plow. Send the trucks
around the coast with cargoes of ice cream and jewels.

A beach slopes down into Blue Carpet Sea;
boats drop anchor in the bay. In the south
volcanoes rumble; in the north
a train wreck blocks the bridge.
What happens next?
We've Thrown the Roads,
and so we make the rules.

Inventing the Tactoscope

Somewhere in my yard there's a spot,
a spot the size of a flickering thought,
where no one's foot has ever walked.

Somewhere on my skin there's an inch,
an inch the size of a tiny pink pinch,
where no one's hand has ever touched.

I imagine a tool
that lets me see
the empty cool
of those deserted places,

that lets me sink with one warm toe
into that lonely spot of yard;
that lets me lay a fingertip
onto that chilly inch of skin.

I imagine a tool
  called a tactoscope.

So Delicious
It Makes You Want to Dance

Call 911! My pants are on fire!
My allowance is burning a hole
in my pocket (my mother says)
and that's just how it feels.

All the way to Bellevue Avenue,
I feel its heat, keep patting it there
as my right thigh comes up,
up, up with each turn of the pedals.

Where will I go? What will it be?
Johnson's Hardware, where the counter
is a wall of candy—candy on racks
stacked from your feet to your teeth?

Or Willey's Drugstore, where the limeade
is green, sweet and icy in its paper cup,
where you can browse the comic books
from your tall spinning stool at the bar?

No—this Saturday I'm steering towards
the Belle Bakery, where the hairnet ladies
take my dimes as politely as dollars,
rustling waxed paper around my

overflowing-with-snowy-
    white-whipped-cream-
    glittering-with-sweet-
    little-sugar-crystals-
    spiral-cone-of-flaky
        pastry called a
        polka roll!

Birdseed

I held
a handful of birdseed
smooth and curved
like tiny beaks   then
I stretched out my arm
and flung it
into the air.

The birdseeds sailed
rust and tan
black and wheat
as though they already
had wings.

They landed   lightly
on raw soil
windowsills

and in the forks
of trees   and wherever
the birdseeds fell   birds
began to grow.

First the bony feet
clawed out
digging down like roots
then the legs began
to sprout   and soon
round bodies budded
leafy wings
unfurled   and then

while I watched
the heads
sleek or crested
dull or shocking bright
blinked eyes
like rainshined fruit.

I planted birdseeds.

Launch

Crocuses are rocketing
    inch by inch
        out of the crumbled earth

the yellows aim for the sun
the purples push   toward deep space

        and inside
little astronauts in orange suits
    cock their ruffled helmets
                    toward spring

Singing the Swing

push back   run forward
    lift into the seat   you're up and away
lean back   rock forward
    reach out with your toes   bend at the knees

this swing is your glider, your rocket, your wings
louder and higher, sing into the air

fall back   flex forward
    reach for the branches   gather your speed
arc back   pitch forward
    kick at the clouds   holler your flight

this swing is your glider, your rocket, your wings
higher and louder, loop over the sun

swoop back   sail forward
    let loose through your heels   hold safe to the chains
streak back   soar forward
    you're rooted in earth but you're singing the swing

Independence Day Graffiti

Oh say can you see
by the winter's pale light
where I scratched my initials
in the fresh-poured cement

I got off of my bike
while the cars whistled by
found a sharp sturdy stick
squatted by the new sidewalk

And my letters were clear
and my flag wasn't square

all my stars and my stripes
seemed to ripple in air

Oh say does my snow-spangled banner yet wave?
Yes, my mark is still there since the day I was brave!

There, Yet

Buckled in back, I'm ready to travel.
I'm not the driver but I plan my own trips;
not the navigator but I read my own maps:

the black map of the pavement;
the broken map of white and yellow lines;
the slow map of the sidewalks.

I follow the trail of leaves in the gutter;
I count the crossing wires, the reds and greens;
I measure how far from here to there.

The car, my mother's chat, my sister's radio—
they roll on, but I've arrived.
I stop to explore my own destinations:

a toppling house,
a thrashing field,
a still puddle of glittering gravel—

the beginnings
of little worlds.

How to Run Away

Take money. Pack light. Coast your bike
down the fastest hill in the neighborhood.
The one by the Baptist church is good.

Claim a weeping willow: plunge through
hanging curtains to find a private room.
The swish of long leaves keeps you company.

Or lie under a cedar with triple trunks
capturing air and space above you.
Its needles make a pungent carpet.

Or climb a dense magnolia. There are
leathery leaves to hide you from enemies,
fuzzy grenades to lob through the branches.

Then go shopping. You don't need much:
saltines, peanut butter, a carton of milk.
Your finger makes a perfect knife.

Now move in and build your nest.
Hang your bag on a twiggy hook.

Stay. Eat. Read your book.
Stay until you know they're worried.
Stay until you miss your brother.
Stay until the shadows cool your mood.

Then pump your book, your bag, your bike
back up that hardest hill
toward home.

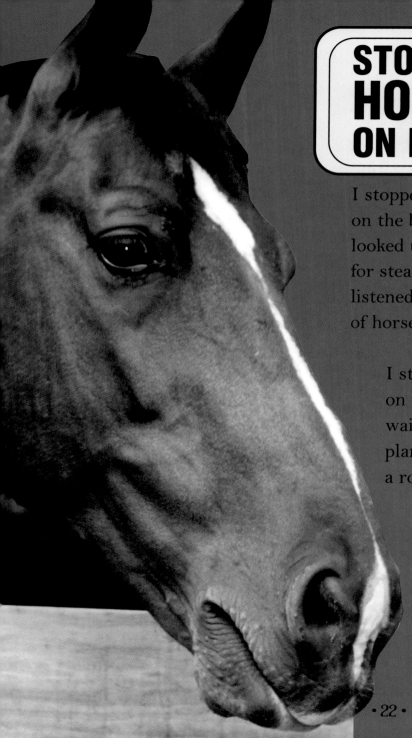

STOP FOR HORSES ON BRIDGE

I stopped for horses
on the bridge—
looked up and down the pebbled path
for steamy velvet muzzles,
listened for the clatter-clop
of horseshoes on the boards.

I stopped for horses
on the bridge—
waited for a whiff of hay and stable,
planned to lay my hand against
a rounded wall of horse.

I stopped for horses
on the bridge—
but horses never came.

What I Wanted and What I Got

A whole new country, Canada!   No,
not a country; a province called Ontario!   No,
not a province, an island—
just an island in a lake with a rocky muddy shore.

An adventure on white water in canoes!   No,
not an adventure; a hike, with boots, packs and trail mix! No,
not a hike; a walk—
just a wander by the shore on a high-grown path.

A bear and her cubs in the top of a tree!   No,
not a bear; a snake of shiny diamonds rippling in the grass!   No,
not a snake; a toe—
just a stubbed toe in sandals and blood on a rock.

A rock to heft with two hands,
a greyish rock in the shape of a fish.   No,
not a rock—a fossil!

A fish's body turned to rock,
a kissing mouth frozen shut,
a ribbed fin on a stony side,
many thousand years old.

A treasure.   Yes,
a treasure surprised by a bleeding toe
on a wander on an island in Ontario.

DEEP END

blow your bubbles out and
s
  i
   n
    k
to the bottom

    eyes   wide open

hair   like   seagrass   riding   little swells

heavy heavy limbs   weightless
                    in the water

    curl
    like
    a creature
    into its shell

hang   in the dazzled
            white world

                      top
                    the
                  to
rolling   up
    cool and hollow   back

Down Under Florida

Lying on the sandy beach
    on the sandy dry backs
  of the giant elephants

Look around and see
    the trunks of the palm trees
    the trunks of the elephants
  stretching to the sky

Listen to the breeze in
    the wild green palm leaves
    the wild green reef water
  shooting from the trunks
  of the sandy elephants

Backseat Breeze

The sun has set.
The singing's over for today;
the fighting ends in truce.
Real driving has begun.

The highway leads us
into the night.
Up front my father steers,
my mother snoozes.

In back my brother sleeps.
But under my frayed blanket
I listen to the dark,
listen to the sound

of the breeze rushing in,
taste it tingling across my
salty, sunburned skin:
warm skin, cool breeze.

I am somewhere, moving, no place,
eyes closed, quiet, lively
night breeze rushing, washing over
my summer self, curled in the backseat.

Rooftop

The roof, the roof!
Over above us evening the clouds—

a platform for diving into the sky
into the radiant gloom of the moon
    we climb and we rise
    from the tarry bloom
on the roof—

a table for dining out on the night
out on the towering stoop of the world
    and the milk winds swoon
    in our dizzy hair
on the roof—

a bandstand for jiving under the heights
under the music of furious blue
    we spin and we sparkle
    too close to the edge
on the roof!

The Moon Moves

I move:
the moon moves.

She meets me over by the shed,
glowing, knowing, hushly rolling
past the dozing vegetable bed.

I move:
the moon moves.

I ride the streets—make any choice
of left or right—and she's still there,
keening in her oyster voice.

I move:
the moon moves.

My smaller wheels turn toward the field.
She follows on her one huge wheel,
yellowing through the darkening leaves.

I stop:
the moon stops.

She waits and watches, ever shines
two hundred thousand miles away,
calling—telling me she's mine.

The Skin Giver
for Satchel

The night after you fall
and scrape your knee--
    the Skin Giver floats
    through your window,
    invisible like God,
    to give you what you lost.

    The place where you fell
    and scraped your knee--
        the Skin Giver goes there,
        hovering over the ground,
        gathering like berries
        the bits of what you lost.

        She brings them in a silken bag
        while you sleep--
            breathing over her buttery breath
            to make them stick
            when she touches
            the spot you thought you lost.

Thinking Wrinkles

I saw a picture of a brain today—
a wet, gray helmet
of wrinkles and folds,
a squish of soft tissue
caught on a background of black.

Now I'm lying in bed, working my way
in and out, over and under,
through the tunnels and
canyons and fissures
that squiggle and squirm in my skull,

And I wonder how something so gray,
so hidden and still,
so ugly and dull,
will dance with the rowdy scarlet sparkle
    of all my dreams tonight.

Falling

A yawn is a wide-open yes to sleep.
I pray the Lord my soul to keep . . .

from leaping out my gaping mouth.
Morning, noon and night fly south

and light upon baredozing toes.
Tickle tickle little nose,

how I wonder what this wind
is sweeping out or sucking in.

My teeth float down in a feathery heap . . .
Yes to the wide-open yawn of sleep.